D0005512

80 GOLDEN WAYS
TO GOOD LUCK

'SARVSHRI' DR. NITIN PARAKH
B.E. CIVIL (Hons.), C. Eng. (I), AMIE, AIV, DBM, Ph. D.
Chartered Engineer, Approved Valuer.
(Gold Medallist)

and
MRS. SEEMA PARAKH
B.A. (Psychology)

NAVNEET PUBLICATIONS (INDIA) LIMITED

Price : Rs. 50.00

G 1021

First Edition : December, 2000.

Publishers : **NAVNEET PUBLICATIONS (INDIA) LIMITED**

Bhavani Shankar Road, Dadar, Mumbai – 400 028.
e-mail : npil@navneet.com

Website : www.navneet.com • www.connectschool.com

Disclaimer : This book describes information & techniques, which have been used throughout the orient for many years. The information detailed in this book, is to the author's and co-author's best knowledge and experiences, and are no claims for their absolute effectiveness. They are to be used by the readers at their own discretion & liability. It may or may not be beneficial depending on one's stage of development. The use of the material offered in this book is totally at the reader's own responsibility and the author, co-author, publisher and printer of this book are not responsible or liable in any manner whatsoever.

This book is available in :

English, Hindi, Marathi, Gujarati, Bengali, Malayalam, Telugu, Tamil, Oriya and Kannada languages.

Published by : Navneet Publications (I) Ltd., Dantali, Gujarat.
Printed at : Paramount Litho & Offset Works, Mumbai – 400 011.
0404

Opinions, Comments & Best Wishes of Some Eminent People

"My best wishes for the success of your book on Feng Shui, with warm regards."

- **Amitabh Bachchan** (Film Actor)

✳

"Wishing your new book venture, a lot of success !"

- **Chandrachur Singh** (Film Actor)

✳

"Our heartiest congratulations on the launch of your Feng Shui Book."

- **Bhagyashree & Himalay** (Film Artists)

✳

"Dr. Nitin Parakh is one of the best Feng Shui and Vaastu experts in the country today! I am sure his new book will be extremely useful to readers. My best wishes for the successful launching of the book."

- **J. K. Gupta** (Chief Comm. of I. T., Retd.)

✳

"Feng Shui is an amazing Science and in my opinion, Dr. Parakh is one of the best exponents of this Science."

- **S.V. Pillai** (ex. Chairman & M.D. Pfizer Ltd.)

✳

"Dr. Nitin Parakh is a highly successful Feng Shui consultant, but still, very down to earth as a person."

- **Gautam Goradia** (C.E.O. Karsondas Exports)

✳

"You are a very successful Feng Shui and Vaastu Consultant, I wish your new book venture, even better success."

- **Sanjay Chabria** (Director - Club Aquaria)

✳

"Dr Parakh, in my opinion is a very knowledgeable Feng Shui & Vaastu expert, and a very friendly person."

- **Mr. Bedi** (L.G. Polymers, of L.G. Group, Korea)

✳

*"He is in great demand and rightly so ! 'He is the **Best** !' In my opinion, he is a valuable friend and a perfect guide. His mere presence can bring about a lot of change in one's life."*

- **Dr. Manish Bansal,** Jt. M.D., R.G. Stone Clinic
(Mumbai, Delhi, Chennai)

✳

"My heartfelt Best wishes, for the success of your new book, God bless !"

- **Manoj Kumar** (Film Maker & Actor)

PREFACE

For the past many years, I have been working on a detailed book on Feng Shui, but the constraints of time posed by my busy schedule, very much delayed the project.

Meanwhile, my wife suggested that I should write a book with small easy tips for the common man, which he can easily use in his house. That is where the idea of this book took seed. My wife is a great help and inspiration to me, and under my training, over the years, her knowledge of Feng Shui increased considerably. She is the co-writer of this book, and has actually done a lot of ground work for this book, under my guidance.

I hope the readers will benefit greatly from this book, and solve their smaller type of problems as regards the subject easily.

— **Dr. Nitin Parakh**

DETAILS OF PROFESSIONAL FENG SHUI
QUALIFICATIONS OF DR. NITIN PARAKH

1. Graduated in the highly prestigious 'MASTER PRACTITIONER COURSE' from Lillian Too Institute of Feng Shui' at Malaysia.

2. Qualified in the advanced 'PRACTITIONER'S LEVEL 1 COURSE' from the 'Wind & Water Geomancy Centre', Singapore.

3. Studied the 'XUAN KONG FENG SHUI COURSE' - Flying Stars (all 4 units) from 'Yap Cheng Hai Feng Shui Centre of Excellence', Malaysia.

4. Studied ELEMENTARY, INTERMEDIATE AND ADVANCED level Flying Star Feng Shui Courses from Master Joseph Yu's Feng Shui Research Centre, Canada.

5. Qualified in advanced level FLYING STAR FENG SHUI after completing the prestigious 'MASTER CLASS' with Master Joseph Yu, the world's leading authority on FLYING STAR FENG SHUI.

6. One of the few illustrious individuals of the world to be awarded the extremely prestigious 'HIGHER DIPLOMA IN FENG SHUI' by Master Joseph Yu-Canada, after passing the examinations.

7. 'Sarvshri' Dr. Nitin Parakh is one of the few select individuals of the world to receive official recognition as 'FENG SHUI PRACTITIONER' from the Feng Shui Research Centre, Canada, after passing the exams.

8. Completed the workshop on 'GEOPATHIC STRESS' conducted by Master Healer 'Christan Hummel' – INSTITUTE OF METAPHYSICAL STUDIES (USA).

9. Member of the 'FENG SHUI SOCIETY' London (U.K.)

DETAILS OF PROFESSIONAL FENG SHUI
QUALIFICATIONS OF MRS. SEEMA PARAKH

1. Completed the course 'PRACTICAL FENG SHUI FOR MODERN LIVING' conducted by the 'Wind & Water Geomancy Centre', Singapore.

2. Qualified in the advanced 'PRACTITIONER'S LEVEL 1 COURSE' from the 'Wind & Water Geomancy Centre', Singapore.

3. Received training for many years under her husband, Sarvshri DR. NITIN PARAKH, India's leading Feng Shui Master & the country's top level authority on 'FLYING STARS FENG SHUI' & 'EIGHT MANSIONS FENG SHUI'.

4. Completed the workshop on 'GEOPATHIC STRESS' conducted by Master Healer 'Christan Hummel' – INSTITUTE OF METAPHYSICAL STUDIES, (USA)

THIS BOOK IS DEDICATED

TO OUR PARENTS AND

TO OUR TWO LOVELY DAUGHTERS

KANIKA & ANUSHKA

CONTENTS

A   (Introduction to Feng Shui)

These days you hear everyone talking about Feng Shui and its ease and effectiveness! People often ask me whether Feng Shui is the only thing that influences a person's luck. The answer is a definite 'No'! But of course, I would not hesitate to say that Feng Shui correction, is the easiest way to <u>enhance</u> your personal luck!. There is a great philosophy behind this, called the 'Trinity of Luck'. There are three types of lucks (1) Heaven Luck, (2) Earth Luck, (3) Mankind Luck. Heaven Luck is the luck you are born with i.e. the influence of stars and planets on your destiny or the retribution or reward you receive for the deeds of your past life. This type of luck is very difficult to change. Mankind luck is the luck that you draw, by really working hard with devotion and dedication i.e. 'Karma'. This is the general assumption that each person would do his best. Earth luck is the luck that you draw from the places you live and work in. This part of the Trinity of Luck is the easiest to correct and can be totally turned in your favour! This is where Feng Shui comes in. The most followed school (system) in Feng Shui is the compass school which is mainly based on a combination of the 'Lo-shu'

4	9	2
3	5	7
8	1	6

The Lo-shu Magic Square

Magic square and the "Pa-Kua' grid : The Lo-shu square consists of numbers 1 to 9, each number used only once. You may add the numbers in any of the horizontal or vertical line or diagonally, and the answer is always 15! The Pa-Kua grid is a grid of 8 life aspirations. This grid is shown below. People quite often tell me that they know from the articles they read, or from some other similar sources, that there are specific areas in their house corresponding to wealth, career, fame, children, elders, helpful people, knowledge and marriage. But the problem is that they don't know **where** these areas are exactly located in their house. No one has so far written about it. Today, I am **revealing** this to the readers ! This is something they can easily use to assess their house on their own. The 8 life aspirations are located in different compass directions of your house, and this is shown clearly on the Pa-Kua diagram that I have drawn.

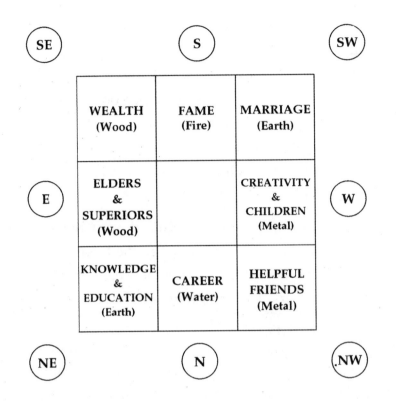

PA - KUA (with directionology)

Example: Fame area is in the south zone of your house, wealth corner is south-east, marriage corner is south-west, etc. Readers can use this grid and place it over the plan of their house to roughly assess their house. e.g. if there is a toilet in the fame area or a cut in it, then you may suffer from ill fame or bad name. If there is a cut in the north zone of your house or if there is a toilet or kitchen in that zone, then your career will have difficulties ! A kitchen / toilet in the area of helpful friends results in not having any mentors or helpful people around you, in your difficult times. Such effects will be visible, but this is not everything. There are certain lucky and unlucky areas and directions for each person in the house. This set of lucky and unlucky directions and locations for each person is calculated astrologically from the person's date of birth and hence certain directions are lucky for some people and unlucky for others. One man's food can be another man's poison !

Each location on the Pa-Kua of your house also has an element attached to it. , e.g., the fame area is in the south and its element is fire. Hence, the placement of a fountain or a fish tank here will have bad results, as water destroys fire. Placement of plants in this location is good as wood enhances fire! Placement of red colour articles also is good here, as the colour red is symbolic of fire. The general wealth corner is the south-east corner of your home and the element here is wood You may enhance it by placing four healthy Jade plants. Avoid any metal objects like scissors, knives, etc. on display here as metal destroys (cuts) wood. Apart from this, another important location, a "Sheng chi" direction, i.e. prosperity location, exists in each house but this varies from person to person. This is calculated from their date of birth according to Feng Shui astrology.

Detailed personal astrological calculations are beyond the scope of this book and form a part of a professional Feng Shui audit of a place. Such an audit by a highly experienced Feng Shui consultant is very necessary in case of serious problems in a house, but minor problems can be easily corrected and the situation can be improved by following easy measures detailed in this book.

Directions, Elements, Colours and Enhancing Objects

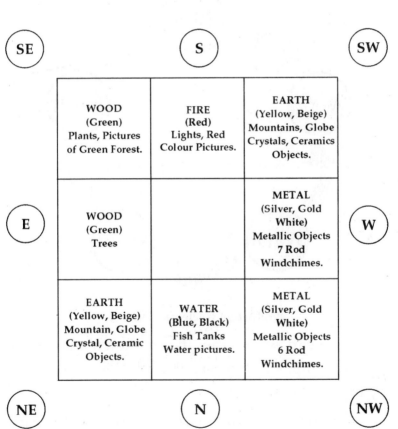

SE		S		SW
	WOOD (Green) Plants, Pictures of Green Forest.	FIRE (Red) Lights, Red Colour Pictures.	EARTH (Yellow, Beige) Mountains, Globe Crystals, Ceramics Objects.	
E	WOOD (Green) Trees		METAL (Silver, Gold White) Metallic Objects 7 Rod Windchimes.	W
	EARTH (Yellow, Beige) Mountain, Globe Crystal, Ceramic Objects.	WATER (Blue, Black) Fish Tanks Water pictures.	METAL (Silver, Gold White) Metallic Objects 6 Rod Windchimes.	
NE		N		NW

Cycle of Elements :

According to Feng Shui, there are five elements in nature. These are wood, fire, earth, metal and water.

These elements are inter-related in two ways, which means that there are two types of cycles of these elements. The productive cycle and the destructive cycle.

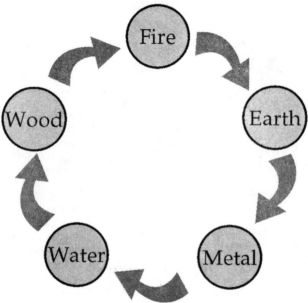

Productive Cycle of Elements

You can see in the above sketch that wood produces fire, which means that you can produce fire by burning wood.

Fire in turn produces earth, because the fire burns and creates ash (earth).

Earth produces metal, because metal is mined from the earth.

Metal produces water; this is said because metal can be melted and then it acquires liquid state like water.

Water produces wood because by watering only we can grow plants !

A beginner may take a while to understand the cycle of elements, but once you understand it properly, it is very easy to use it for enhancing your house.

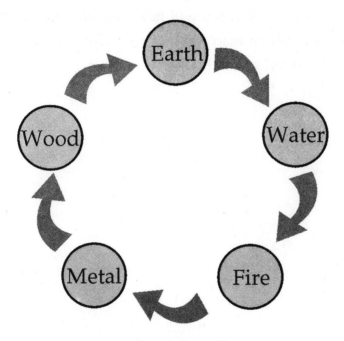

Destructive Cycle of Elements

In the above destructive cycle diagram, you can easily see that wood destroys earth, because trees grow on earth and suck away all minerals and leave the earth barren.

Fire destroys metal, because fire melts the metal.

Earth destroys water, because earth (mud) absorbs all the water, when it rains.

Metal destroys woods, because implements made of sharp metal can cut the trees.

Water destroys fire, because water can put off any fire.

Understanding these two cycles of production and destruction of elements will help you understand the reasoning behind many enhancing measures that have been described in this book.

*   *   *

1

Front Door Should not Face a Toilet

The location of a toilet in a house is very important as it is a negative area. There should be no toilet facing the main door of the house. If there is a toilet opposite the main door, its door should be changed immediately. This can be done by closing the toilet door, and making the entrance to the toilet from another wall or another room.

If this change is not possible you can have a solid barrier between the front door and the toilet, which will prevent the good energy entering through the main door, from draining down the toilet. Make sure that the barrier should be solid enough. A curtain as a barrier will not do.

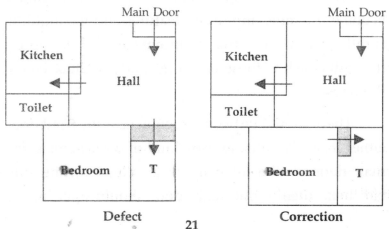

Another defect is to have a toilet in close proximity of the main door. In this case, the bad energy from the toilet mixes with the good energy entering from the main door. The correction is to shift the door of the toilet to any other side, away from the main door.

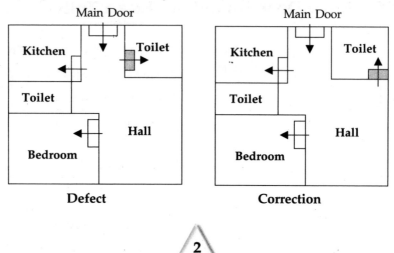

Defect   Correction

2

Front Door to be Free of Obstruction

According to Feng Shui the main door of the house is one of the most important features and it should be rightly placed. It is this main entrance of the house through which all the good energy and good luck enters the house.

There should be no obstruction near the front door either inside or outside. Any kind of obstacle near the main door could result in all the good luck turning into bad luck. Ideally, the main door should open into a bright spacious room or a small foyer with no obstructions like a shoe rack, etc. near the door. There should be no clutter near the door.

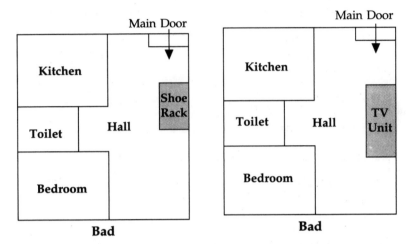

Another type of obstruction in front of your main door is the presence of a column (pillar) in front of the main door. This is a very serious type of defect and should be immediately corrected, by shifting your door.

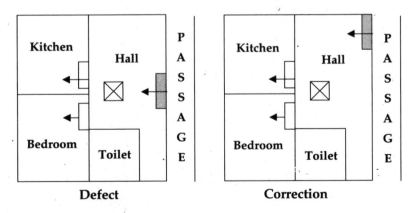

No Obstructions Outside Your Main Door

In my long years of practice, I have come across many bad houses and people suffering due to the defects in their houses. One of the most serious defects that I have seen in flats, is an obstructing wall just opposite your main door, on the outside.

The apartment I have drawn in the example shown below, had the main door facing the staircase of the building.

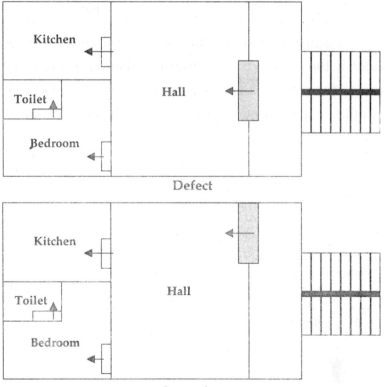

Defect

Correction

The middle wall between the upward and downward flights of the building staircase was bang opposite, and right in the centre, outside the main door of the apartment. This is a very serious obstruction right outside the main door, and I have observed, in my practice that such a defect causes very serious consequences for the inmates of the house.

No Mirror Opposite the Front Door

During my practice, I have witnessed on many occasions, that mirrors are kept directly opposite the main door of the house. Such a practice is very harmful as this results in the reflecting back of the good *chi* (energy) that enters from the main door. It is reflected back and escapes out of the door !

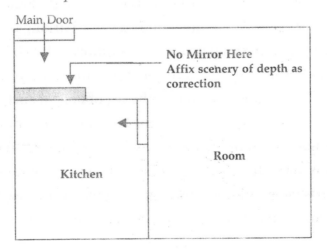

I have even come across cases when the client had been advised by an inexperienced consultant to affix a big mirror opposite the main door because the entrance had a blank wall opposite it !

An entrance to a blank wall is bad, but this type of correction to create depth by means of a mirror, is very wrong in my opinion. The right correction, is to affix a scenery of depth on the opposite wall. It can be a scene of a road or path meandering and going deep into the forest, mainly to create the feeling of depth symbolically.

(Avoid Flats Above Stilt Floor)

Nowadays in all big cities, due to the non-availability of space around the buildings, there is a tendency of constructing stilt floors for parking of cars. These open parking spaces are supported by columns only. Avoid buying flats on the first floor of such buildings because the life of the occupants of such flats is not very stable, This happens because such buildings lack solid foundation and there is a free flow of energy below these flats. This is not a very serious defect but, if possible avoid the situation. You may purchase flats on the second floor or above in such buildings.

(Avoid Three Doors in One Line)

Three doors in one line formation is a deadly physical Feng Shui defect because it allows *chi* to funnel across at great speed through these doors and the occupants of the last room, at the end, get badly affected due to this defect.

An easy correction is to shift the middle door on one side to break this 3 door effect.

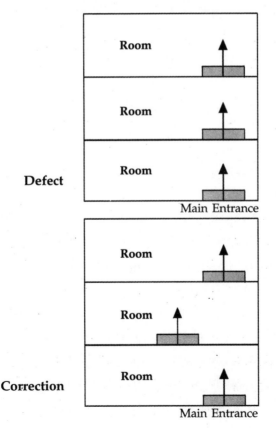

(Avoid Top Floor Flats)

Before buying a flat on the top floor of any building, do check up, whether the building's overhead water storage tank is located over your chosen flat or not. If it is located right above your chosen flat, please do not buy that flat. If the overhead tank is located elsewhere, and not right above your chosen flat, you may buy that flat. The reason to avoid flats with overhead water tanks right over your flat, especially right over your bedroom, is that, water at a height is considered dangerous in Feng Shui and sleeping right under it, is considered risky.

8

(Mirrors Reflecting the Dining Table)

Large mirrors or wall mirrors have been proved to be an excellent source of energy especially in the dining room. This is a very good way of bringing in Feng Shui luck for 'eating'. Mirror reflecting the dining table creates an impression of doubling of the food on the table. This kind of set up may not enhance directly your wealth and riches, but it definitely ensures that the family will never lack food. You can hang a picture of delicious food in the dining room or place a bowl with fresh fruits on the table. Your refrigerator should be well stocked at all times. All this symbolises the availability of food in the house.

Mirrors near the dining table are good, but mirrors near the stove are very bad Feng Shui. You may get injured in such a case and even your life could be in danger. Mirrors reflecting the dining table enhance good fortunes, whereas mirrors reflecting the cooking gas cylinder or the stove, can be fatal.

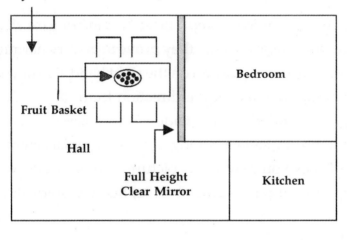

9

(Aquarium with Goldfish)

A great way of enhancing good luck in the house, is by keeping some goldfish in an aquarium or fish bowl. You should keep nine goldfish, out of which eight should be red or golden in colour and one should be black. If your goldfish die, do not worry, just get some more and replace them. It is also believed that when a fish dies in your home, it takes some of the bad luck away with it, which otherwise would have befallen a member of the family.

Avoid keeping goldfish in the bedroom, or in the kitchen or in the toilet. It can lead to some material losses. The best place to keep an aquarium is in the living room, and the right direction is in the East, South-east, or North.

Water features, if kept correctly, can bring excellent luck. But if kept wrongly they prove to be very harmful. Never place an aquarium on the right hand side of your main door (i.e. taking the direction from the inside of the house and looking outside). This causes the man of the house to have a roving eye. As a replacement of real fishes you may use a picture of blue water, with dolphins jumping upwards in it., But real goldfish are the best.

(Display Auspicious Symbols)

The Chinese of olden times liked to display auspicious writings and symbols in their homes, which bring them luck. We Indians can display auspicious symbols such as Swastik and Om as these symbolise extreme good fortune. Writings and symbols can be hung as special paintings, or carved on to wood blocks or furniture.

I have used the symbol of the Swastik, Om and Trishul together many times in my practice and have found them very useful. It was given to me by a Reiki teacher, Rekha Kale. You can affix this symbol on both sides of your main door on the outside as a protection for your house. You can carry this on your person, by affixing it in sticker form on your diary, etc. for personal protection and good luck.

Swastik - Om - Trishul

(Avoid Scenes of War and Violence)

Never display pictures of violence. There should be no paintings or pictures depicting violence anywhere in your house especially in the South-west corner, as it is the corner of relationships. If there is a picture of war or wild animals in the South-west, it could have ill effects on your relations with other family members.

Displaying scenes of the Mahabharata or weapons which symbolises violence could lead to arguments in the family and disturbed relationships with your loved ones. In my experience of thousands of cases, I have observed that among joint families most often these pictures are a cause of the mother-in-law vs daughter-in-law conflicts.

People have, many times, asked me as to what is wrong with the scene of Mahabharata in which Shri Krishna imparts 'Bhagwad Geeta' to Arjuna. The answer is that, here Arjun is all geared up for the war and having such a picture in the house, probably causes our subconscious mind always to be ready to fight !

Hang Feng Shui
Coins or Bells on the Door Handles

Hanging coins on the door handles is an excellent way to bring money luck into your home. You can hang three old Chinese coins, tied with a red thread or a

Bells   **Chinese Coins**

ribbon on the door handle. This benefits all the members of the house. The coins should be hung on <u>the inside of the door and not outside</u>. Please do not go to the extreme and hang coins on each and every door of your house. Hanging coins on the main door is enough.

You can even hang a small bell on the door handle <u>on the outside</u>. This symbolises good luck coming into the house, where as coins symbolise wealth which has already come into the house. You should not hang any coins on the back door, as the back door represents the way through which something goes away from you.

Avoid Cactus and Bonsai: Keep Jade Plants

The cactus plants should never be kept inside an office or a house. Its little thorns give out negative energy and act as poison arrows which can be very harmful. Avoid placing bonsai plants in the home or office. Though they may look very nice and beautiful, they represent stunted growth which adversely affects one's business, career, studies, etc.

Bonsai (Bad)　　　　　　　　**Jade Plant (Good)**

It is very auspicious to keep jade plants in the house especially in the South-east corner which is the direction for wealth. This energises the wealth luck in your house.

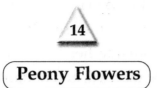

Peony Flowers

In Feng Shui, flowers are widely used for enhancing certain sectors in the house. The peony flower is generally associated with women. If a family consists of mainly girls, and they are of marrigeable age, then hanging a large picture of many peonies in the living room will be very effective. The best place to hang a painting of peonies, is the living room, and it will bring the required marriage luck to the family. Real peony flowers can also 'be used instead of a painting. They should be kept in the 'SW' corner of the living room.

Peony Flower

If a girl is single and of marriageable age, and wants to find a good husband, then she should put the picture of a peony just outside her bedroom door. But if a woman is already married, and hangs the painting of a peony inside the bedroom, it could make her husband develop a roving eye and also to develop interest outside the marriage. Hence, the best place to hang a peony painting is the living room, and not the bedroom. This activates the romance luck in one's life.

15

Avoid Dried Flowers

Plants are a useful source of Feng Shui. When used in an office or a home they create excellent *yang* energy and bring good luck into the home.

Fresh flowers can be displayed in the house, but as soon as they start drying or fading they should be removed or replaced with fresh ones. Fresh flowers symbolise life, whereas dried flowers symbolise death and give out *yin* energy. However precious a loved one may be, but still his dead body is not kept in the house. Similarly, anything that represents death or *yin* energy should not be kept inside the house.

Placing plants in the living room or dining room is better than placing them in the bedroom. But keeping plants in the bedroom of a sick person is extremely good. Artificial i.e. plastic or silk flowers, can be used instead of fresh ones. Dry arrangement of flowers such as pot pourri, etc. should be avoided.

Hi-Fi Appliances

With the progress of technology we have more and more hi-fi equipment in the market by each passing day. Houses also possess more hi-fi equipment now. These appliances can be beneficial to the house if placed in the right location. The West wall or the West corner in the living room is the best place to keep these hi-fi appliances, and this will bring good luck to the residents.

Since the hi-fi equipment symbolises the metal element, it is best suited in the West, as the West corner of your living room is governed by the element metal.

Television sets, if kept in the bedroom, should not face the bed directly, as it acts as a reflective surface, like a mirror, and can create misunderstandings among the couples. This is extremely bad Feng Shui, and gives out negative energy.

If one feels like keeping a television set in the bedroom one should keep the set covered when it is not in use.

(Avoid Open Shelves)

Many people love reading books and they also take pride in possessing them. The habit, per se, is very good. But books, when kept in open shelves create *shar chi* or 'killing breath' which is bad for the occupant of the room. Open book shelves whether in the office or in the home are like knives, which give out negative energy and is bad Feng Shui.

Such open book shelves can result in the occupant of the room falling ill and at times the illness may even prove fatal. This effect may not be visible immediately, but will manifest itself over a period of time. The best way to correct this is by having doors, on all the shelves. Keep the shelves covered and not exposed. This will reduce the bad effects of the open shelves.

Open book shelves

(No Mirrors in the Bedroom)

Mirrors give out a kind of energy that can be either extremely good or extremely bad according to the location where it is fixed.

Mirrors are a taboo in the bedroom. There should be no mirrors facing the bed since it creates major disturbances in the marital relationships of the couple. It could even lead to a third person entering an otherwise healthy relationship. The negative effects of mirrors can be reduced by keeping it covered, or by having built-in mirrors inside cupboards.

Mirrors reflecting the sleeping couple, may even cause a divorce. So the mirrors should be kept out of sight during the night and there should be no mirrors on the ceiling either.

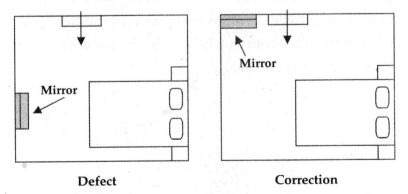

Defect   Correction

Don't Sleep on Double Bed with two Separate Mattresses

In my long experience of practising this wonderful science, I have come across cases of all kinds. Many times I get couples on the verge of divorce coming to me to try fengshui out, as a last ditch effort, before they officially part ways !

I remember an interesting case of a doctor couple who could not get along ! I saw that they had a double bed, but two separate mattresses on it. This is very bad because sleeping on separate mattresses leads to separation !

Always have a double bed with a single piece bed/ mattress only. Sleeping of married couples on <u>two separate single beds</u> is not as bad, and becomes sometimes necessary, when their personal lucky directions differ completely, and both of them happen to be earning members.

Avoid Sleeping in Front of the Door

In China, the position in which a person's feet directly face the door, is considered a death position. In fact, dead bodies are kept in this position, which is considered good for them. But at the same time, it is an extremely harmful position for the living.

While sleeping it is necessary to make sure that neither a person's head, nor his feet, are directly in front of the door. This is a *yin* position, and can have extremely bad effects on the person. It is best to place the bed either to the right or left of the door.

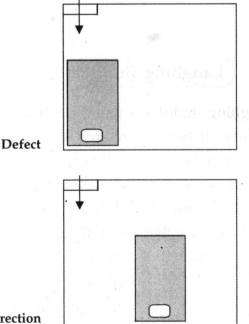

Defect

Correction

(No Aquariums in Bedrooms)

Never keep a water feature i.e. an aquarium or a small fish bowl or a scene of waterfall or sea beach, etc. in the bedroom. This affects the relationship between the married couples badly, hence it is to be essentially avoided. If you happen to have any such water feature or water picture in your bedroom, please get rid of it immediately. Sometimes, the career area (north) falls in a bedroom and in such a case, it should be enhanced by metal objects and not a water feature. Metal objects enhance the water element of the north.

(Laughing Buddha)

The laughing Buddha is regarded as one of the gods of wealth. It brings prosperity, success and financial gains in the house. The location of placing the laughing Buddha is important. It has to sit at some 30" approximate height and should be facing directly the main door. The energy that enters the house from the main door is greeted by the laughing Buddha and the energy is activated, and turns highly prosperous.

Laughing Buddha

If this location is not possible, the next best place to keep the Buddha, is on a side table, or a corner table which is diagonally opposite to front door and facing the door. It is not advisable to keep the laughing Buddha in the bedroom or in the dining room. This god of wealth is not worshipped or prayed to but just displayed, as its presence is purely symbolic and auspicious.

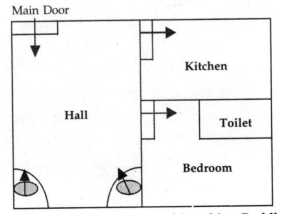

Good Positions and Facing of Laughing Buddha

Three-Legged Frog

The three-legged frog is considered very lucky. It usually has one or three coins in its mouth. The position of the three-legged frog with a coin in its mouth, is very important. It is to be placed anywhere near your main door on the inside and it should look inwards, as if it has just entered your house with the money ! Do not ever place this frog with the coin facing, i.e. looking at your main door, as this symbolises money going out of the house !

Never place frogs inside the kitchens and toilet as this is to invite bad luck.

Three Legged Frog

Happy Family Photo for Good Relationship

One of the best and the easiest methods of creating a sense of family togetherness, is to hang a large family photo in the South-west corner in the living room. Every member of the family should be included in the picture, and to symbolise happiness, each one in the photograph should have a smiling countenance.

Happy Family Photo

This is especially effective in the Indian joint family concept, where mother-in-law *vs* daughter-in-law tiffs are common.

Hang a photo of both together, and smiling, and in a loving happy pose, to enhance their relationship.

A married couple should hang a photograph of the two of them together in a happy loving pose, in the south-west corner of their bedroom to enhance their love and affection.

(Keep Brooms Hidden)

Brooms and mops are used in each and every household for cleaning and keeping the place tidy. They also symbolise the cleaning away of the bad or negative energies that enter the home. Brooms exposed to view are considered inauspicious, so they should be kept hidden.

Avoid exposed brooms especially in the dining room, since it signifies that the food and the earnings of the family are being swept away.

If you keep a broom outside your house in the upside down position and facing your main door, it gives protection against intruders. This can be done during the night, but the broom should be kept hidden, and out of sight during the day.

(Mopping the House with Salt Water)

Salt water is used for purifying a place, or a thing like quartz crystals. It helps in removing the negativity that a place may be having. Mopping a house daily, with salt water is considered auspicious. Five spoons of unrefined sea salt can be added to the mop water. This reduces the negative effects or the negative energies of a place.

(Clutter Clearing)

Many people have the habit of keeping unwanted things and stuffing up their spaces with such things. They neither use it nor throw it away. This is clutter.

Example:

(a) It may be the old clothes that you store, hoping for them to come back to fashion, or which have been given as gifts - expensive ones, but you don't like them, because they are of synthetic material. You don't wear them because of one reason or the other, but you do not throw them away either.

(b) Old magazines, paper, clippings from newspapers,

old books which you hope may be useful some day but actually more than five years have passed without you having read/used them, even once.

(c)   Chipped or broken show pieces, etc.

(d)   Old video cassettes and old audio cassettes.

(e)   Old appliances which don't work anymore.

(f)   Watches and clocks, that are not working.

(g)   Junk and old newspapers.

(h)   Very old account and record books, more than 15 years old.

(i)   Mental clutter - old emotional and traumatic memories.

Remove all the clutter from your life, if you want to progress. Clutter holds people back, each piece of junk attaches an invisible string to you, and all this hampers progress, because each of these hoarded things occupies a space (like megabyte of computer memory) of your mind. We have only limited space in the mind and we should not clutter it up. Get rid of all physical and mental clutter, and see how free, comfortable and happy you feel ! Just as the same way a Yogi, gets rid of social ties for spiritual progress, you should get rid of your extra physical possessions, for materialistic progress !

Another thing you can do after clutter clearing is to light up incense sticks daily in the house, for space clearing. You may even ring a bell after *pooja*, all over the house - if you like.

Crystal Balls for Good Relationships and Romance

The South-west corner of the house is connected to love, romance and relationships. This area has the earth element. The best way to energise this area is with the use of two genuine natural quartz crystals. The activation of the South-west corner of your bedroom with real crystals, ensures great harmony and happiness in relationships with loved ones.

If this is done in the living room, relationships within the whole family get enhanced.

Crystal Ball

The genuine quartz crystals, are to be purified. They should be kept in salt water, for at least one week to remove any negative energies attached to them. The real quartz crystals are especially effective, because they can be programmed with thought forms. The procedure is as follows:

> Immerse each crystal ball, in a glass of water with four spoons of unrefined sea salt. After purification for a week in salt water, wash the crystal in flowing tap water and keep it on a ceramic saucer, out, in early morning sunlight for three hours. During this time practise forming a picture in your mind, that your whole family is together and smiling i.e. happy together.

If you want your daughter to be married off in a happy matrimony, imagine a picture that the marriage is already taking place and she is smiling (happy) in that picture. Once you are easily able to visualise this, lift the crystal from the sunlight and place it on your left palm, and cover it with the right palm, close your eyes and conjure up the picture in to your mind and let it stay for a few seconds. Your crystal is now programmed. Hang it in the South-west corner of the house, or in your daughter's bedroom as the case may be. I have found real crystal balls, and crystal pyramids, etc. to be very effective in thousands of cases I dealt with, during my professional experience.

Yellow Flowers in Cream Colour Ceramic Vase

This is an easy way to enhance relationships amongst the members of the house. Keep a cream coloured ceramic vase and keep artificial yellow coloured flowers in it, in the South-west corner of the house - this is the area of relationships and keeping this type of coloured flowers here, acts in enhancing relationships. The colours yellow and cream symbolise the earth element.

Growing an Orange Plant

An orange or lime tree, with ripe fruits, symbolises good luck and prosperity. Such plants are usually kept at the entrances to doors of homes and office buildings. The significance of bright red oranges symbolises gold and it is regarded as extreme good fortune to have a lot of oranges around, during the new year. Grow an orange plant in your garden, in the South-east because this is the area of your house that signifies wealth. Having a healthy, fruiting orange plant there, is very auspicious.

In apartments you can keep an artificial orange plant in the South-east (wealth area), to enhance prosperity. These days you get artificial orange plants which look as original and beautiful as the real ones.

Lovebirds for Romance

According to Western tradition, love birds are considered as one of the main symbols of love, romance and fidelity. Whereas in Chinese culture mandarin ducks are symbolic of love and romance in young couples. These ducks can be placed in the South-west corner of the house or South-west corner of the

Mandarin Ducks

bedroom, since South-west is the area for relationships and romance. This enhances your love life.

If you are single, and looking forward to getting married, you can hang a painting of these ducks or place a pair of ducks in your bedroom. But please make sure that you put a pair, not one or three, since one implies that you will remain single, and three implies, that there could be the entry of a third person in the marriage.

If you want to attract the opposite sex, then make sure that you place a male and a female duck in a pair. Not two males or two females.

Love Birds

The love birds are as effective as the mandarin ducks. The birds can also be displayed as a painting or a picture. Do not display birds in cages as this is bad Feng Shui. The caged bird symbolises the inability to fly or lack of ambition.

Chandeliers in South-West

The South-west corner of your house is of the earth element and is attached to the "marriage and relationships" aspect of life. If you happen to have your drawing room here at this corner, make use of the situation and install a lead crystal chandelier here, and keep it on, every evening for at least two hours. This enhances the earth element of this area tremendously and will result in harmonising the relationships within family members, as well as enhancing marital prospects of unmarried members in the family.

Chandelier

Crystal Glass Bowl with Coins in 'NW'

The North-west area of your house corresponds to the master of the house, the bread winner ! The element of this area is metal. You can enhance the metal energy of this area by keeping a crystal bowl full of real metal coins. This should be preferably kept hidden from general public view.

Keep Toilet Doors Always Closed

In olden times, houses always had the toilets located outside the main house. This was a very healthy practice because toilets are the places where we throw all our body's waste. It is full of toxins, bacteria, etc. The remnants of these remain in the drain water of the toilet, and hence the toilet is a source of bad energy in every house. It always affects badly, the area of life aspirations of the Pa-Kua, wherever it is located in the house. Hence, a toilet should always be, at least designed to be located in the personal unlucky areas of the main earning member of the family. A detailed description of this is beyond the scope of the present book. This forms part of the eight-mansions-formula, of the Compass school of Feng Shui.

Anyway one has to accept the fact, that apartments today, do have attached toilets, hence the least you can do is to keep the toilet lid closed all the time except when it is being used. Likewise, the toilet door should remain closed except during the times of entry and exit. Then the bad energy of the toilet, does not mix with the good energy of the house. Also please use phenyl liberally to disinfect your toilets regularly, preferably daily or at least weekly.

Another important point to remember is, not to overdecorate your toilets. These days, there is a tendency among interior designers to decorate the toilets expensively. It is better to keep them simple.

Kitchen Clean and Burners Unblocked

The uncared-for burners get clogged with oil and grime. Always periodically unclog the burners and keep them clean. Keep your kitchen also, always clean and tidy.

(Water and Fire in the Kitchen)

Never place water and fire i.e. the sink and the burners in your kitchen, adjacent to each other or exactly opposite to each other.

The reason for this is that, fire & water are absolute opposites, as is evident from the destructive cycle of elements, described earlier, in this book.

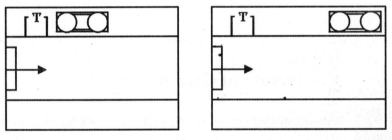

Defect A   Correction A

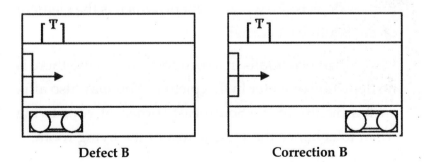

Defect B   Correction B

Eating Together Daily

Make it a point to tell your family members, that at least one meal will be had together. Fix up the time for the meal and wait for sometime if required, for all family members to be on the dining table to eat together. This practice enhances relationships. Remember, that a family that eats together, stays together !

Picture of Greenery in 'SE'

A good enhancer of prosperity, is a scene of green forest without hills, in the South-east corner (wealth corner) of your house. This is because, this kind of picture depicts the wood element, which is the element of the South-east corner.

If this corner falls in a bedroom, make sure there is no depiction of water in this picture. You may also affix such a picture in the South-east corner, of your living room to enhance the wealth area of the living room.

Knives, Scissors are Bad Gifts

Knives, forks, scissors, etc. serve as poison arrows which send bad energies when pointed directly towards a person. Never place sharp, pointed objects facing yourself, or facing someone else.

While presenting a gift to someone, keep in mind never to give sharp objects as gifts. These sharp objects give out hostile energies which could create frictions between friends. It can result in the end of a friendship which is flourishing otherwise. To avoid unpleasantness in a relationship, avoid the presence of sharp, pointed objects around you.

Crystals in North-East for Education Luck

The north-east corner of your house is the one that corresponds to education and knowledge. The element of this area is earth. To enhance the performance of your children in their exams, hang crystal balls (preferably eight in Numbers) in the north-east corner.

(Children's Pictures in West)

West area of your house corresponds to 'Children and Creativity'. If you display pictures of your children here on the wall, you will be enhancing their energy and luck.

(Don't Sit with Open Window Behind You)

In your office, never sit with an open window right behind your back, as this causes a drain of energy and also reduces confidence and causes stress, especially if your office is on the ground floor with a road-view outside the window, because your back becomes exposed.

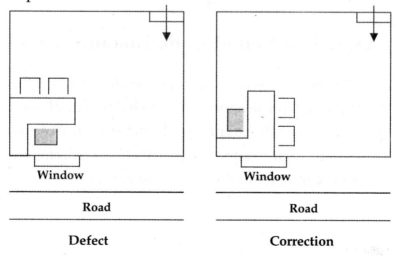

Window	Window
Road	Road
Defect	**Correction**

Boss's/Mentor's Picture

The north-west area of your house corresponds to the 'helpful people' or 'benefactors'. In this area, if you keep a picture of your boss, you will enhance the sympathy that you get from him, or if your boss is antagonistic in his attitude towards you, keeping his picture in this area of your house will make him become little more sympathetic towards you.

Bowl of Salt in Toilets

Toilets are the place, where we throw our body's waste, and this waste contain toxins, bacteria, etc. Hence the toilets, wherever they are located inside the house, are always a source of bad energy. Keep a bowl full of unrefined sea salt in every toilet of the house on the window sill, as salt absorbs the negative energy. You may periodically replace the salt in the bowl, as and when it gets wet and soggy.

(Avoid Leaky Taps & Choked Drains)

In Feng Shui, water is wealth! So, if in your house there is any tap which is continuously leaking, please repair it immediately, as this would result in draining of your money. Similarly, choked up toilet drains should also be immediately got cleared up and declogged.

(Windchimes)

Windchimes are an excellent source of enhancing good luck in the house. The number of rods in a wind chime and the material by which a windchime is made are important.

Windchimes

You are not supposed to hang windchimes, anywhere and everywhere, in a home. Their location is extremely important. The best place to hang a six-rod windchime is in the North-West corner of your living room, since the governing element of this corner is metal and wind chimes are symbolic of metal. They are used to enhance good luck and also to reduce bad luck.

If you want to deflect a poison arrow, you should use a five-rod windchime and it also suppresses bad luck. A seven-rod windchime can be hung in the west zone of your house.

Owner's Picture in South

If you are fortunate enough to have an office of your own, make sure you frame a good photograph of yourself (owner) in a Red bordered frame and fix it in the south zone of your office. This is a good tip to enhance your name and goodwill.

You may even print your company's name or product's brand name in red letters on a pink background or light green background and stick it in the south zone of your office. This will enhance the goodwill and name of your company or brand.

The reason for the above is that, the element of the south is fire, and the aspiration attached to it, is 'Fame'.

Here, we should note that the colour red is symbolic of the fire element.

Ship with Gold Coins

The sailing ship is considered as a symbol of high achievement in one's work and success in business. A model ship can be displayed in the office or home. While displaying, make sure that the ship is sailing inwards, and not outwards. The ship should be sailing towards the inside of the office. If the sailing ship appears to be facing the door, or sailing away, it symbolises that all your opportunities are going away, and you may have losses in business.

Another important thing to note, is the kind of model ship you install. If you display the model of the Titanic, which, as you know sank, it could result in your business sinking too!! So display the right kind of ship. The next step you can do, is to put a few imitation gold coins in the ship, which is symbolic of good fortune coming your way and is very auspicious. If you cannot find imitation gold coins, then you can just put some coins and money in the ship.

Avoid Ceramic / Earthen Ware in the North

The north of the house is of 'Water' element and in the destructive cycle of elements, the earth element destroys water. Hence, ceramic or earthenware should not be kept in this area of your house, as this is harmful to the water energy of this area and as such can affect your 'career' negatively.

Items made of crystalware and chandeliers made of lead glass crystal, are also not to be placed, in this area of North.

Genuine quartz crystal balls, are also not to be hung in this area.

Globe in North-East for Education and Knowledge

The placement of a globe, depicting the whole planet Earth, is also a good enhancer of education and knowledge, if kept in the north-east corner of your house, because the element of this area is the earth.

(Chinese Coins for Money Luck)

The use of Chinese coins to activate money luck is very effective. You can take three Chinese coins and tie them with a red thread. This you can keep in your purse or wallet. It symbolises a continuous source of income for an individual. You can use three coins, rather than four or five, since the number three itself is very auspicious.

Chinese Coins

Tying the coins with a red thread, is necessary as the red thread activates the coins, and gives out *yang* energy.

These coins given as gifts to someone is wonderful. You can even add the coins to the gifts and presents that you are giving, since it is considered very auspicious.

These old Chinese coins, are round coins with square holes in the centre.

(Metal Vase with White Flowers in North)

The north area of your house corresponds to your "Career and Opportunities." Enhance this area with the placement of a metal vase preferably, wrought iron or steel vase, with artificial white coloured flowers.

(Musical Clocks)

You should go and select a good musical clock and buy it and fix it in your house. The music should be a soft tune and pleasing to the ear. Remember Feng Shui is about balance, hence too loud a sound becomes noise.

Remember, to never hang a clock above any door or doorway!

Avoid Blue Colour Pictures and Water Scenery in South

The south area of your house is of the 'Fire' element, and is connected to the 'Fame' aspirations of life on the Pa-Kua. In the destructive cycle of elements, 'Water' destroys 'Fire'. Hence, scenes of water in this area, are harmful for your goodwill and name, and also blue coloured articles kept here are better removed, because the colour blue, is symbolic of the water element.

Round-off Sharp Edges and Corners

Sharp corners and edges of furniture should be smoothly rounded-off, as these are sources of *Shar chi* (bad energy). When you make new furniture, always make sure that all furniture is rectangular but with soft rounded corners and edges. Whenever possible, also round-off the exposed column and beam edges.

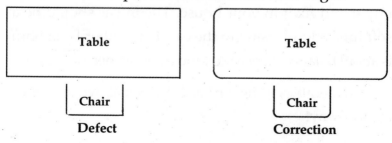

Seven-Rod Windchime in West

The west area of your house, corresponding to Children and Creativity, has the number 'seven' attached to it on the Lo-Shu grid, hence hanging a seven-rod metal windchime here enhances the energy of this area strongly.

Here, we should note that the element of the west corner is metal.

Red Picture or Object in South

The south zone of your house, is the one that corresponds to the 'Fame' aspiration in life. The element of this area is fire and you can enhance your fame, name and goodwill by hanging a red colour picture, in this area or keeping a red colour object here, because the colour red is symbolic of the fire element.

Three Lucky Coins in Cash Box

Old Chinese coins are one of the most effective means of enhancing wealth, luck and prosperity. Three Chinese coins, tied with a red thread can be kept in the cash box for increasing your wealth.

Another excellent way to improve the sales in your shops is by installing a mirror which reflects your cash box. Mirrors are an effective way of improving your Feng Shui luck. Mirrors can be put anywhere in the shop, except where the main door is being reflected, because this will be very harmful. If the mirror reflects the main door of a shop, rather than the cash register, all the energy entering the shop will be reflected, and directly go out, as also all the good fortune can go out.

Mirrors reflecting the goods in a shop symbolises that the goods are doubled, and so is the turnover of the shop. The shop appears to be well-stocked at all the times, and when the cash box is reflected, it symbolises wealth and good fortune, being doubled.

You may even tie the three lucky Chinese coins with the red thread over your cash register book, and all important account books, etc.

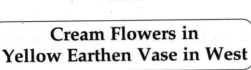

Cream Flowers in
Yellow Earthen Vase in West

The west area of the house, has the metal element and metal is produced by earth in the productive cycle of elements. Hence, keeping a yellow coloured ceramic or earthen vase in the west, with artificial cream coloured flowers will enhance the metal energy of this area and will have benefits on 'Creativity and Children' which is the life aspiration, this west area corresponds to.

Avoid Green Plants in South-West

The south-west corner of your house is of the 'earth' element and is connected to relationship and marriage aspirations. Green plants are of the wood element, and in the destructive cycle of elements, wood destroys earth. The presence of green plants here hence is harmful to the earth energy of this area and can affect relationship badly. It will also reduce marital prospects, If you have already kept green plants in this area of your house, please get rid of them immediately.

Agarbattis for Cleansing Negative Energy

People in every household use agarbattis or incense sticks for worshipping God. Agarbattis give out a lovely fragrance and at the same time have a wonderful effect on the surrounding place. They are extremely useful, as they cleanse the air of negative energies.

Burning of incense sticks creates energy, that purifies the place, and has a calming effect on people. So, burning of agarbattis and incense sticks daily is excellent and very auspicious.

Gayatri Mantra or Sacred Chants

Every morning, after the daily prayers, chant the Gayatri Mantra, or put on a cassette playing this in the house for some time. This fills up the house with good vibrations. You may say sacred chants of your own religion, instead of the Gayatri Mantra, if you are not a Hindu.

Avoid Bright Lights and Red Objects in North-West

There are times in one's life, when a person receives unexpected help from another person, or when one is betrayed by his own people. In Feng Shui, there are ways in which one can enhance the mentor luck, i.e. luck of helpful people in your life.

The North-West, is the corner for mentor luck, and you can energise this corner, by hanging a hollow six-rod windchime made of metal here, since metal is the element of this corner.

Do not place bright lights or chandeliers in the North-West corner of your home, as it is extremely harmful. Red objects symbolise fire, and are bad when kept in the North-West. It can lead to betrayal, and no helpful people around you, when you need them the most.

Avoid Metal Objects and Scissors in 'SE'

The element of the 'SE' is wood, and in the destructive cycle of five elements, metal cuts (destroys) wood. Hence, keeping sharp metal objects like scissors, knives, etc. in this area is harmful to the energy of this area. The negative effect hinders prosperity, because the life aspiration attached to the area is 'wealth'.

Metal Turtle in the North

Place a metal model of a turtle or terrapin in a small bowl of water and keep it in the north zone of your home. The turtle is a good enhancer of longevity and also, in the north, it is an enhancer for career opportunities. You should just keep the model of metal turtle alone, without the water bowl, if you happen to

Metal Turtle

have a bedroom in the north zone of your house, since keeping water in a bedroom is not advisable.

Keeping an actual/real turtle/terrapin, in a small vessel of water, in this area is an even better enhancer, but the metal turtle works well too.

(Curtains for Good Luck)

Curtains and all the upholstery in the house or office, can be designed to suit your personal element, and can bring good luck.

The colour and design on a curtain differ according to its location. Ideally, the curtain should have two layers. The curtains in a west room should be white since the element of this area is metal, which signifies white. Similarly, for a room which is in the north, blue curtains are most suitable, since the element here is water. The south corner of a house can have curtains with a triangular pattern, and red colour; this symbolises the fire element. For an east room which is governed by the element wood, rectangular curtains would be good, and they can be of green colour.

Non-functional Clocks & Appliances

Remove all clocks and watches which are not working from your house. Please get rid of them at the earliest as they are quite harmful.

Many clients tell me that these old clocks have sentimental values for them. I tell them that if it is so, please take care of them, get them repaired and serviced, and keep them in functioning condition.

Don't Sit with Your Back to the Door

One should never sit in an office with one's back to the door, even if this means sacrificing your personal luckiest direction, for a second best one. Sitting with your back to the door, causes back stabbing or cheating or frauds and also lack of control, because the main door is not in your view.

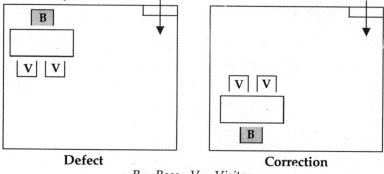

Defect   Correction

B = Boss   V = Visitor

(No Calendars Over, or on Any Doors)

Never hang calendars on the back or front of any doors or doorways, because hanging calendar or clocks over doors or above them, especially above the main door is bad for longevity of the inmates, as it is symbolic of telling you how many days are left in your life!

(Don't Sit Facing a Blank Wall)

Since the advent of computers and Internet in India in a big way, I came across a lot of senior executives of big companies, and even big businessmen sitting, facing a blank wall with a computer screen in front of them. For the visitors, they provide an informal kind of seating

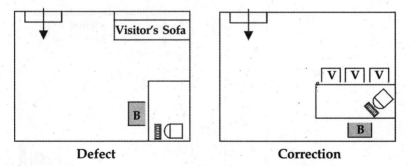

Defect **Correction**

arrangement on a sofa on the side. This is a very unhealthy trend, because the key decision maker is facing a blank wall. He will slowly become a man with short-term thinking, whereas, he needs to be a person, with a long term vision. I am showing this arrangement on the sketch below as well as the correction.

Mountain Behind You for Support

In any office, my suggestion is that the important decision making executives should never sit with their backs to the door, since this almost amounts to betrayal or cheating. I remember an interesting case from my practice. I was once invited by a big advertising agency for a Feng Shui Audit. I checked up the MD's cabin and was surprised to see him facing a wall and sitting with the door of his cabin behind him on one side. The direction he was facing was also astrologically unlucky for him, according to his date of birth.

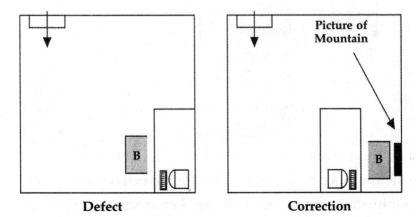

Defect   **Correction**

When I told him that such a sitting arrangement causes cheating or fraud, he was taken aback. He admitted that he had been defrauded for more than a crore of rupees by an employee who handled his accounts !

I told him to change his position and sit with his back to the wall and the door facing him. I received news of improvement in his business very soon.

It is advisable to strengthen the back support by hanging a picture of a mountain on the wall just behind your seat. The best mountain type, is the one resembling a turtle. The mountain behind your back, is symbolic of strong support behind you, and increases the feeling of self-confidence. People with weak will and lack of self-confidence, should definitely make use of this measure for their benefit.

Dragon for Good Luck

The dragon is a symbol of excellent *Yang* energy. You can energise your office by keeping the model of a dragon on the east side of your office. The east is the direction associated with this celestial creature. The element of the east is wood, hence a dragon carved out of wood is very good. You may even use dragons made of ceramic or crystal, but don't keep metal ones because metal destroys the wood element, of the east.

The dragon is a symbol of tremendous yang energy. Hence, it is very good to display pictures of dragons in the east of restaurants, shops, departmental stores, etc., wherever lot of energy and movement is desirable.

Dragon

Avoid the display of the dragon model, or its pictures in the bedrooms because these are places where we intend to give rest to our tired bodies, and there, a symbol as *yang* as the dragon, is not desirable.

Phoenix for Success

The Phoenix is one of the celestial animals of Feng Shui and Chinese mythology. It symbolises the luck of wish fulfilment. The Phoenix is very effective in activating the south corner. To energise your luck, look for symbols, paintings or pictures of the Phoenix, and affix those on the south corner of your office. The Phoenix image at a distance on the south also symbolises farsightedness, which is essential for any intelligent businessman.

Phoenix

(Horse-shoe for Good Fortune)

The horse-shoe is considered a lucky charm in the West as well as in India ! The shape of the horse-shoe describes the ideal land configuration of Feng Shui, hence it is considered a favourable shape as per Feng Shui also.

In India, traditionally, people considered the horse-shoe as a lucky charm and use it by affixing it above their main doors for protection and good luck.

It is said that the real horse-shoe which a horse has worn, and which has been energised by the horse's galloping, is really lucky! If you happen to find such a horse-shoe, you can affix it above your main door on the outside above the door-frame. The ideal way is to affix it with its prongs pointing downwards.

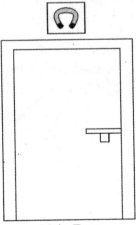

Main Door

Since the horse-shoe is of the metal element, avoid its usage, for east and south-east facing doors. It is especially effective for west, north-west and north facing doors.

(Bamboos for Luck)

Bamboo plants are considered a very potent symbol of longevity in Feng Shui ! Bamboos represent strong growth even in the midst of adverse circumstances, and symbolise the ability to withstand all kinds of stormy weather !

The bamboo plant symbolises long life and good health. The bamboo plant also symbolises good fortune. Hence, you may energise your office or house even with the picture of a bamboo plant. Hanging a bamboo stem in your retail shop can create a good protection *chi* for your shop. The business will symbolically survive harsh times, and flourish during good times, like the bamboo plant ! You may use a pair of bamboo stems tied with red thread on the wall, opposite the main entry of the shop. They should be open at both ends and can be approximately six-inch to eight-inch long.

(Telephone and Fax at Right Place)

The telephone and the fax machines are communication devices. They are the harbingers of business to you. Whenever the phone rings, you get excited at the opportunity of a customer calling you up, to give business to you, or asking for your goods or services. It is always desirable to have customers, who are sympathetic to you, and are almost like mentors to you. The telephone and fax machines are of the metal element. Hence, due to both the above reasons, I advocate the placement of the telephones and fax machines, in the north-west corner of the office, as far as possible.

Here we should note that the north-west is the area of helpful people, and its element is metal.

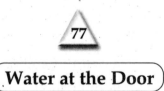

(Water at the Door)

A water feature at the door is considered a very lucky feature. It is especially useful for north facing, east facing and south-east facing doors. The water feature must be carefully kept, only on one side of the door and that also to the left side only, i.e. to the left, when you are standing inside the house, and looking outside. This is shown in the sketch drawn below for more clarity.

This type of water feature, kept as above, is considered very lucky, and gives a lot of benefit. It may be in the form of a fish tank, or even, a picture of blue water with dolphins jumping upwards, playfully.

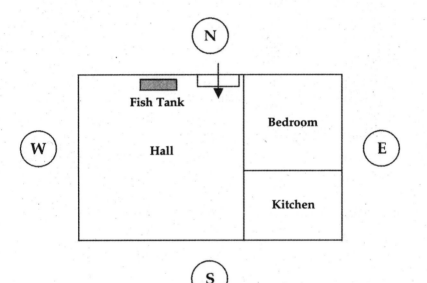

Always remember that we should never keep the water feature to the right of the door, as this could cause a side effect. It could cause the man of the house to develop a roving eye, or even the entry of a third person in your marriage.

Never keep water, on both sides of the door, because water on both sides of the door is like tears in the two eyes.

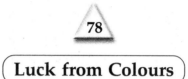

Luck from Colours

Whenever you are renovating or repainting your house, you can energise it, with the use of colours as per the chart given below. You can paint rooms in particular colours, according to the element of the area, or the element that produces it. You have to be careful to avoid the colours that go against (destroy) the element of the area. For e.g., avoid blue colour or black colour in south side room. Avoid green colour in the north-east room.

Corner	Element	Best Colour	Good Colour	Bad Colour
North-East	Earth	Yellow, Beige	Red, Orange	Green
North	Water	Blue, Black	White, Silver	Yellow, Beige
North-West	Metal	White, Silver	Yellow, Beige	Red, Orange
West	Metal	White, Grey	Yellow, Beige	Red, Orange
South-West	Earth	Yellow, Beige	Red, Orange	Green
South	Fire	Red, Orange	Green	Blue, Black
South-East	Wood	Light Green	Blue, Black	White, Silver
East	Wood	Green	Blue, Black	White, Silver
Centre	Earth	Yellow, Beige	Red, Orange	Green

(Couples without a Baby)

A baby, is like a lamp of bright light, in your life. It is indeed very sad, that many couples are childless, despite apparently no problem with either spouse. To my mind, it is the effect of the fast paced modern city life and pollution, especially in a city like Mumbai. The stress and the effects of air pollution, etc., probably reduces the heat of the womb, and fertilisation is difficult. Feng Shui offers ways and means to enhance chances of conception. Each person has a lucky direction (personalised), which is his *nien yen* direction. My method to enhance chances of conception, include allocating a room in the *nien yen* location for the husband, and sleeping with his head in his *nien yen* direction.

The detailed astrological calculations for the same are beyond the scope of a simple book like this. Anyway, very often, couples unable to conceive are hit by poison arrows of some kind in their bedroom, or at their main door. Check your main door and see if there is any obstruction outside it, or a poison arrow, hitting it. In an apartment, the main door may have a poison arrow of a sharp column or a wall edge pointing at the main door. Sleeping below a beam, or having a column edge pointing towards you in the bedroom, is also a poison arrow. Protect yourself from all such poison arrows to enhance your chances of conception. Play soft romantic music while sleeping especially when trying for a child and be relaxed.

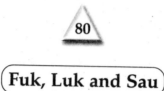

(Fuk, Luk and Sau)

You will find statues of these three Chinese gods in all Chinese homes. Fuk, Luk and Sau are the gods of wealth, high rank and longevity respectively. The statues of these three gods are rarely worshipped. Their presence is merely symbolic. Their presence in the house is considered to be very very lucky.

Luk   Fuk   Sau

Fuk is the god of wealth, and is taller than the other two gods. He is generally placed in the centre.

Luk is the god of high rank and authority. Sau is the god of longevity. He has a round head which is almost bald.

Fuk, Luk & Sau together represent the three most important types of good fortunes.

They are displayed together, and their presence is said to ensure wealth, authority, respect, long life and good health.

*   *   *

C   Limitations

This book is meant for the common man to try to help himself in his various aspects of life like health, wealth, relationships, etc. The procedures and the methods described in this book are sufficient enough for small improvements to solve minor difficulties in life by energising the house. These 80 ways are like vitamins of medical science. A generally healthy person, without any serious or major illness, can improve his health with vitamins, but vitamins are not of much use in case of any serious or major illness, wherein a detailed treatment becomes necessary. This is the analogy I can give you. If you have any serious or major problem in life, a detailed Feng Shui audit of your home or office becomes necessary, but always be on guard that you do not go about consulting any amateur or inexperienced consultant, just because he charges less. If you have a serious problem in life, it is better not to be pennywise and pound foolish! Consult a good Feng Shui Consultant who is highly experienced, because there is no substitute for experience. Remember that a genuinely experienced good Feng Shui expert is worth his weight in gold. His fees probably would be repaid many times over, by the benefit you stand to gain from his expert guidance.

Another important thing is that, only from long years of experience, does a Consultant really know, what works well in Feng Shui and what doesn't. As a lot of original Feng Shui literature in China was destroyed by one of the emperors during his regime, the first hand experience of the Feng Shui consultant is of supreme importance. This emperor had made use of Feng Shui knowledge for his palace and strengthened himself, and did not want his detractors to benefit from it, and hence he got a lot of original books of literature destroyed, and circulated books with fake knowledge about Feng Shui. These kinds of books still find their way into the modern world. Though there are so many schools (systems) in Feng Shui, only experience teaches one as to, what works best, under particular circumstances.

D   Where to Get these Items?

The author has had a lot of people asking him where to buy real genuine quartz crystals? Where do you get a particular picture of depth etc.? Many times his clients have told him that they are unable to buy them anywhere. Hence, the co-author, Mrs. Seema Parakh, has arranged for stocking a collection of these items.

If you wish to buy some of these items and are unable to buy them anywhere, you may contact Tel. No. **670 0911** or personally come to the address given on page 92, to buy these items (subject to availability).

Address:

G.F. Classique, Gulmohar Main Road,

Juhu Scheme, Mumbai 400 049.

Imp. Note: 1. Timings-Afternoon 2.00 p.m. to 5.00 p.m.
only.

2. Closed on Sundays & Public Holidays.

3. Please do not call up on any other telephone
numbers of the authors for enquiries
regarding these items.

Landmark: Junction of Juhu Lane & Gulmohar Road.

How to Reach:

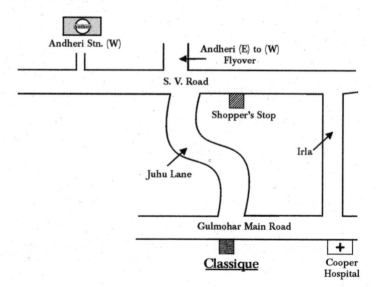

Outstation readers can write to us, along with a self-addressed, stamped envelope. We will mail them the pricelist and they can then send a DD so that we can parcel the respective items, as per their order.

E | Details about Professionally Consulting the Author

The author of this book 'SARVSHRI' Dr. NITIN PARAKH is a highly experienced and much sought after Consultant, and if you wish to consult him, you may contact any one of the following Tel. Nos.:

Tel. : 620 3900

Cellular : 98201 47625

e-mail : nitinpar@rediffmail.com

Notes:

1. The above Nos. are only for securing an appointment. Please do not call· up on these numbers, for any other type of enquiries, or enquiries regarding any information in this book, etc. as they will not be responded due to constraints of time, because Dr. Parakh runs a very busy schedule of professional Feng Shui Consultations for his clients.

2. For professional consultations, you will have to take an appointment, a minimum of 3 months in advance as he is generally booked in advance for this much time, during any part of the year. He generally undertakes only 2 visits in a day, because he does not like to compromise on the time he gives to each place during a Feng Shui Audit. A professional Feng Shui Audit of even a small 3 BHK

apartment generally takes around 3 hours, because he attends and observes even the smallest detail of the house, and draws a sketch of the house, showing the required corrections and enhancements.

3. During a Feng Shui Audit, Dr. Parakh takes the date of birth of all the residents of the family, especially the main earning member of the house and works out according to Feng Shui astrology, the <u>lucky & unlucky</u> personal directions for each person and then advises lucky rooms, head side position and facing directions, for each member of the family, for enhancement of their personal luck.

    He also works out astrologically the birth element of each person in the house, as the cures advised in each person's room should be compatible to their personal elements. This is how he achieves the best results.

4. The various sectors pertaining to the eight life aspirations like wealth, health, relationships, etc. are checked up and wrong placements are corrected, and enhancement of sectors are advised, using methods described in this book, among other things.

5. The main door of the house is extremely important and whatsoever be the reasons, the main door has to be <u>lucky</u> for the main earning member of

the family, based on his date of birth. This is absolutely important from the prosperity point of view. If such is not the case, its directional re-orientation is sometimes advised, by Mr. Parakh, during the Feng Shui audit of the premises.

6. There is also a time dimension involved, meaning that directions, and various locations of the house also pass through, good and bad phases of time (flying stars). This also is taken into consideration many a times during the Feng Shui audit of the premises.

*   *   *

OFFICE ADDRESSES

Mumbai : *Regd. Office* : Navneet Bhavan, B. S. Rd., Dadar, Mumbai – 400 028. (Tel. 5662 6565)

Ahmadabad : Navneet House, Gurukul Road, Memnagar, Ahmadabad – 380 052. (Tel. 810 5000)

Bangalore : Sri Balaji's, No. 12, 3rd Cross Road, Malleswaram, Bangalore – 560 003. (Tel. 2346 5740)

Bhopal : Navneet Sadan, E7/728, Arera Colony, Shahpura, Bhopal – 462 016. (Tel. 527 8544)

Chennai : 30, Shriram Nagar, North Street, Alwarpet, Chennai – 600 018. (Tel. 2434 6404)

Delhi : 2E/23, Orion Plaza, Jhandewalan Extn; New Delhi – 110 055. (Tel. 2361 0170)

Hyderabad : Bldg. No. 3-2-331, Somasundaram St., Secunderabad – 500 025. (Tel. 5531 7348)

Kolkata : Newar Bhavan, 1st Floor, Chowringhee Road, Kolkata – 700 020. (Tel. 2223 2497)

Nagpur : 63, Opp. Shivaji Science College, Congress Nagar, Nagpur – 440 012. (Tel. 252 1522)

Nashik : Dharmaraj Plaza, Old Gangapur Naka, Gangapur Road, Nashik – 422 005. (Tel. 231 0627)

Navsari : 3/C, Arvind Nagar Society, Lunsikui Road, Navsari – 396 445. (Tel. 244 186)

Patna : 1st Floor, 36-D, Sahdeo Mahto Marg, Srikrishnapuri, Patna – 800 001. (Tel. 220 4921)

Pune : Sita Park, 18, Shivaji Nagar, Near Bharat Eng. School, Pune – 411 005. (Tel. 2553 6364)

Surat : 1, Shree Vallabh Complex, Kotwal Street, Nanpara, Surat – 395 001. (Tel. 2346 3927)

Vadodara : F/1, Vaidya Vatika, Sardar Bhuvan Khancho, Vadodara – 390 001.

SHOWROOM ADDRESSES

MUMBAI ● **Mahavir Stores,** Shop No. 4, Ajanta Apts., P. M. Road, Santacruz (W) ✦ 2649 4457 ● **Navneet Showroom,** Near Sharadashram, B. S. Road, Dadar (W) ✦ 5662 6545 ● **Romsons,** 1-2, Vira Shopping Centre, Station Road, Dombivli (E) ✦ 286 1143 ● **Mahavir Collection,** Shop No. 7, Near Voltas Pokhran Road No. 2, Thane ✦ 2539 8001

AHMADABAD ● **A.R. Book Treasure,** C.G.Road, Near Municipal Market, Navarangpura ✦ 656 3020 ● **M/s Chheda Agencies,** Navneet House, Opp. Gurukul Road, Memnagar ✦ 810 5000 ● **Supreme Educational Gallery,** 30, Shubh Complex, Rajasthan Hospital Road, Shahibaug ✦ 285 9151

RAJKOT ● **Navneet Showroom,** Shivam Complex, Ground Floor, Dr. Yagnik Road, Opp. Jaganath Temple, Rajkot.

BELGAUM ● **Aum Trading Corporation,** G-1&4, Radio Complex, Shivaji Road✦ 422 678

COIMBATORE ● **Kesarishih Vallabhdas,** 197 Ramalingam (West), R. S. Puram ✦ 247 0937

DHARWAD ● Pragati Udyog, 30 Mahishi Road ✦ 244 4025

GODHRA ● **Puja Enterprises,** Shop Nos. 1, 2, & 3, Unique Complex Basement, Prabha Rd., Godhra ✦ 02672-249497

HYDERABAD ● **Glorious Enterprises,** 4-3-548/1, Need's Arcade, Bogulkunta Cross Road, Hyderabad ✦ 2475 3219

MADURAI ● **Shah's XPressions,** 95, East Veli Street ✦ 0452-233 5275

NAGPUR ● **Mangalam,** Shree Vithal Complex, Dhantoli Park, Abhyankar Road, Dhantoli, Nagpur ✦ 254 9476

NASHIK ● **Mahavir's,** 4, Dattatreya Darshan, College Road, Nashik ✦ 231 7924

PATNA ● **Gyan Ganga Pvt. Ltd.,** M–2/36, S. K. Puri, Boring Road✦ 226 1956

PUNE ● **Anshuman Collections,** Shop No 6-A, Ashok-Vijay Complex, M. G. Road, Pune-1 ✦ 401 2664 ● **Poona Automobiles,** 177/78, Laxmi Road, Near Belbaug Chowk, Pune-2 ✦ 445 2655

SOLAPUR ● **Jitesh Vastu Bhandar,** Opp. Hotel Anand Bhavan, Manek Chowk Solapur ✦ 0217-274 1061